The principal objective of THE MATHESON TRUST is to promote the study of comparative religion from the point of view of the underlying harmony of the great religious and philosophical traditions of the world. This objective is being pursued through such means as audio-visual media, the support and sponsorship of lecture series and conferences, the creation of a website, collaboration with film production companies and publishing companies as well as the Trust's own series of publications.

The Matheson Monographs cover a wide range of themes within the field of comparative religion: scriptural exegesis in different religious traditions; the modalities of spiritual and contemplative life; in-depth mystical studies of particular religious traditions; broad comparative analyses taking in a series of religious forms; studies of traditional arts, crafts and cosmological science; and contemporary scholarly expositions of religious philosophy and metaphysics. The monographs also comprise translations of both classical and contemporary texts, as well as transcriptions of lectures by, and interviews with, spiritual and scholarly authorities from different religious and philosophical traditions.

The beauty of the Rose teaches the eyes to sigh.

WHEN THE ROSE BLOOMS

WHEN THE ROSE BLOOMS

Spiritual Aphorisms by M. Ali Lakhani
Illustrations by Nigel Jackson

THE MATHESON TRUST
For the Study of Comparative Religion

When the Rose blooms,
the Garden is everywhere.

© M. Ali Lakhani, 2021
Illustrations © Sacred Web Publishing and Nigel Jackson

This first edition published by

The Matheson Trust
PO Box 336
56 Gloucester Road
London SW7 4UB, UK

www.themathesontrust.org

ISBN: 978-1-908092-22-9

All rights reserved. No part of this publication may be reproduced, stored in a retrieval system, or transmitted in any form or by any means, electronic, mechanical, photocopying, recording, or otherwise, without the prior written permission of the Publisher.

British Library Cataloguing-in-Publication Data.
A catalogue record for this book is available from the British Library.

Typeset in Baskerville 10 Pro

Cover: Illustration by Nigel Jackson
Typesetting and design by Susana Marín

CONTENTS

PREFACE *by M. Ali Lakhani* xi
INTRODUCTION: EMBRACING THE SILENCE
by Barry McDonald xiii

SPIRITUAL APHORISMS

- Mystery. 3
- Faith and Certitude 4
- Intelligence and Discernment 5
- Seen and Unseen. 7
- Real and Unreal 9
- Aspects and Vistas 12
- Emptiness and Plenitude 14

- Ego and Awareness 19
- Time and Presence. 21
- Enclosures and Openings 23
- Seeking and Finding. 25
- Effort and Grace 27
- Possibilities and Outcomes 31
- Meaning and Purpose 32

- Ignorance and Vanity 39
- Temptation and Desire. 41
- Struggle and Suffering. 43
- Choices and Consequences 45
- Virtue and Dignity 47
- Repentance and Forgiveness. 50

- Compassion and Mercy 52
- Exile and Longing 59
- Freedom and Captivity. 64
- Hope 67
- Self and Other 68
- Independence and Interdependence . . . 71
- Trust and Dependence 72
- Self-Surrender 73
- Inwardness and Transcendence 79
- Prayer and Silence 81
- Love 84
- Wholeness and Harmony 87
- Serenity. 88
- Transfiguration and Beauty 89
- Union. 90

BIOGRAPHIES OF THE CONTRIBUTORS. 93

ILLUSTRATIONS *by Nigel Jackson*
- The beauty of the rose... ii
- When the rose blooms.... v
- The dragon you slay... xvii
- The key and lamp... 15
- Beware of the panther.... 35
- How night vanishes... 55
- The fires that burn in hell... 75
- The ship of desire... 91
- First, I was a fish.... 95

PREFACE

This book has been long in the making. The aphorisms were written mostly over three decades ago, then left to germinate and grow. Eventually certain groupings suggested themselves. This selection is the result. Though their presentation here suggests an order, they did not emerge that way; so, they can be read sequentially or randomly.

Thank you, Nigel Jackson, for your creative collaboration and beautiful illustrations, rich in symbolism; and Barry McDonald for your encouragement and generous Introduction, written many years ago. And to The Matheson Trust for publishing this book, and to Susana Marín for her design.

Thanks also to my wife, Nazlin, for helping me to weed the Garden and plant deep.

This offering is to the community of Friends—to all who long for the Rose to bloom.

M. Ali Lakhani
March 21, 2021
Vancouver, BC, Canada

INTRODUCTION: EMBRACING THE SILENCE

Who has not known the wonder of seeing the first few stars rising in the dusk? Against the darkening immensity of the sky, though they are very far away they seem to speak of what is most near. In realms of love and pain who has not known treasures lost and found, dreamed and known awakenings that shaped one's life. And who has not felt oneself part of a vast tapestry, too large to see, sewn by a single thread running through all things seen and unseen, without beginning and without end. By such moments we are marked by an invisible, but indelible, ink. Philosophers and poets write with this ink and it is this writing, interwoven of speech and silence, which blossoms and bears fruit in the clarifying beauty of these aphorisms.

The geography of these utterances, each like a signpost, maps a vast and ancient territory in few words. Tracing the frontiers of Prayer and Silence ('If you let the silence within you sing to itself, you will become its song'); Self and Other ('We are merely translations of each other's lives'); Enclosures and Openings ('Immensity threads itself through a needle's eye'); Exile and Longing ('What we cannot hold in our arms, we hold even closer in our dreams'); Possibilities and Outcomes ('The privilege of life is not to open doors, but to choose those by which to enter'); Seen and Unseen ('Does the world disappear when we close our eyes? We are closer than we imagine to what we cannot see'); and Inwardness and Transcendence ('The fire dies into the ashes of its flame'). A voice from the edge of silence is heard throughout this book; it is at turns metaphysical, mystical, moral, practical, wounded, healed, searching and even humorous. This voice is that of the spiritual seeker's heart and mind laid bare and the nearly whispered words are like small whirlpools beckoning the attentive reader into the depths of our shared human experience—and, in those depths, we find God. The drowning to which it calls us means death in life; but it also means life in death.

At their highest points of tension these aphorisms synthesize entire novels, works of philosophy and spirituality, and poetry, into a few chiseled words, often wrought into a single sentence reminiscent of Blake's seeing 'infinity in a grain of sand'. There is a story of an ancient Chinese emperor who held a poetry contest, promising some great treasure for the winning poet. All of the famous poets of the land came from far and wide and offered the emperor their most beautiful poems. One had composed a poem using only a single word, a mysterious word lost in the history of telling this story, and it was the winning entry. The primordial simplicity which must have set that word to music resonates through the pages of this book; one is reminded of the symmetry of snowflakes, illuminating and purifying, dancing in the dark. This simplicity is close to wisdom because simplicity is the essence of unity; and in

INTRODUCTION

the dazzling light of unity, seeing the One in the many, all wisdom is revealed. By extension, one could say that to hear God one must hear the Silence which threads through all of the many forms of sound. Silence, it is said, is a name of the Buddha.

Although I referred above to the frontiers, or themes, traced in this book it is important to note that frontiers are crossed with a single step. The themes merge seamlessly into each other; and by way of utilizing another metaphor, as the whole tapestry contains each individual thread, each thread speaks of the whole. Scholars of various spiritual traditions will no doubt detect elements of Sufism, Zen, Vedanta, and other esoteric schools of thought in these aphorisms; however, the text cannot be pinned down and classified under any specific heading. These utterances are universal in their meaning and appeal, they do not seem to be of any time or place; they speak from a center which is everywhere and nowhere at the same time. They speak to travelers on a timeless journey. One is immediately struck by the authenticity and genuine reality of these words, like jewels lit from within, sparingly used, and often directing the reader to the very precipice of what it is possible to say. 'Silence proclaims silence. Man, however, searches for something to hear'. Listening to these nearly unspoken words, one hears the lilt of sunlight on a flowing stream, the cry of a falling star, or the stories told by a grain of sand. If you cannot hear, then listen more closely. In the depth of your listening there are rewards beyond measure.

Barry McDonald
October 2005

The dragon you slay is a phantom,
but the dragon that slays you is real.

SPIRITUAL
APHORISMS

Mystery

Many things emerge from the Centre,
but the Centre itself does not emerge.

∞

The night has more secrets than the day can tell.

∞

Stars shine, but only in darkness.

∞

Everything recedes into the darkness
from which it comes.

∞

The Word is the breath of Silence.

Faith and Certitude

Receptivity, to those who are not receptive,
is credulity.

❧

Faith is the surrender of intelligence to mystery.

❧

I thought you were a step,
but my foot discovered you were a chasm.

❧

The foot is firm so long as the ground is firm.

❧

The wind can never blow the sky away.

Intelligence and Discernment

Intelligence is the attention needed
to perceive the real.

※

One cannot truly know
something one is not.

※

Knowledge is not the visible,
but the Light that makes it visible.

※

The sightless see the Sun
by knowing its effects.

※

One must stop looking beyond in order to see.

It is through darkness
that one sees the light.

Seen and Unseen

Does the world disappear when we close our eyes?
We are closer than we imagine to what we cannot see.

※

Where can your shadow hide but within?

※

The eyes we lack are not our own.

※

We have been given eyes to see the invisible.

※

The choir of flowers is dumb
only to the ears of the deaf.

There are eyes trapped inside stones,
but we are too blind to see.

An eye that has not learned to see itself
has not learned to see.

The pinhole must become an eye
for the universe to be seen.

I looked for light with light,
but discovered only darkness.

Real and Unreal

The dragon you slay is a phantom,
but the dragon that slays you is real.

❧

Words are not ashes,
though ink is a flame.

❧

The Light casts shadows
the mind deems real.

❧

Light itself is the gift;
all else misses the prize.

❧

Truth has many tongues,
but only one voice.

❧

What is does not cease to be except
in our perception of it.

❧

The water and its wetness are one.

❧

I thought reality was the flame that flickered
till I discovered it was the eye that blinked.

❧

It is the wilting flower that is real.

❧

The dance is not in the dust
but in the wind that swirls the dust.

❧

Dust is only dust, even when
the wind lifts it up to the sky.

❧

The rosebud's fragance
blossoms in the soul.

Aspects and Vistas

The maker of signs made me!

❧

The world appears to the eyes
according to the nature of the eyes.

❧

In every shadow is the beauty of light.

❧

Darkness effaces what light sharpens.

❧

Those who live in the valley do not see
the same mountain as those who scale its peak.

❦

As the garden is in the seed,
so the Beloved is in the world.

❦

Man looks out of a window into a garden,
and the window disappears.
Man looks out of a window into a garden,
and the garden disappears.
Man looks out of a window into a garden,
and the man disappears.

Emptiness and Plenitude

Reality reflects nothing,
yet everything is reflected in it.

※

The heart cannot carry
more than it can yield.

※

It is the flowing water
that keeps the fountain alive.

※

Man is the edge of emptiness:
each moment, emptiness is filled.

The key and lamp are both within.

Ego and Awareness

Am I the flowing
or its source?

❧

Because we open into ourselves,
we never sense the opening.

❧

The temptation to witness the process
diminishes our experience of it.

❧

The veil that separates us is no deeper than ourselves.

❧

Faith is the conviction that enables us
to throw stones at the mirror.

❧

The whole world was in your eyes
until I let them fall from my gaze.

❧

A wintry moon, still, on water.
A snowflake's tremor jolts the mind.

❧

The falcon's shadow startles its prey.

Time and Presence

Memory cannot hold onto what is;
the eyes must discover it afresh in each moment.

☙

The absence into which we return
is always present.

☙

Time is a memory I am learning to forget.

☙

Each moment we discover the emptiness we fill.

☙

No egg hatches before its time.

❧

The sky releases the ocean one drop at a time.

❧

Time opens doors, creating the passage
we ourselves become.

❧

Stitch by stitch, the thread becomes the tapestry.

❧

The vortex quickens, the dregs drain.

❧

In time, the darkness you imagine will be real.

Enclosures and Openings

Life is not an enclosure but an opening.

༄

Immensity threads itself through a needle's eye.

༄

Walls are built from within.

༄

Even a wall becomes a door
when one yearns for it to open.

༄

The heart's door
always opens inward.

❧

All my life I have drawn circles around me,
yet I have never found a place to hide.

❧

Man must become the opening through which to flow.

❧

Our growth is an opening
into the wholeness we contain.

Seeking and Finding

The treasure is not found by opening boxes
but by emerging from the box that is open.

❦

One cannot fully grasp
what one cannot transcend.

❦

Light determines where the shadows hide.

❦

To find oneself is to be discovered!

❦

Man is limited by a desire to manifest the unseen.

❧

Silence proclaims silence.
Man, however, searches for something to hear.

❧

Life is a quest for the footprint
hidden beneath one's own foot.

❧

The eyes encompass the horizon
that the heart discovers within.

Effort and Grace

It is the cupped palm,
not the grasping hand,
that receives water.

❧

No lamp can light the darkness
unless first you light the lamp.

❧

If you are not ready to teach yourself,
you are not ready to learn.

❧

The seed that does not find the flower within,
will never open.

I cannot show you the flower you do not long to see.

The pearl we seek lies deep
in the heart of the diver.

We, who have learned to plant seeds,
must now learn to let them grow.

Some wait for the floor to move
for the dancing to begin!

Man has only to unfurl his sails
to catch the wind that will bring him to the shore.

Truth cannot be plucked;
it has to flower.

The entrance is not by entering
but by being entered.

We are merely matches waiting to be struck.

Man is a bird on a floating log,
in search of wings.

The eyes of love are opened
only by a light unseen.

❧

That within us which is awake, must awaken
that within us which slumbers.

❧

Thoughts are given to those who are ready
to receive.

❧

Love can choose only readiness;
the rest is grace.

❧

Stillness is a means of pursuit,
sometimes the only means we have.

Possibilities and Outcomes

Each opening defines its own possibility.

※

We choose only from the choices we are given.

※

The privilege of life is not to open doors
but to choose those by which to enter.

※

The chosen path is ordained.

※

The world is arranged by a hand one cannot see.

Meaning and Purpose

Man is torn between discovering meaning and inventing its purpose.

❧

Nothing is more profound than simplicity.

❧

As words recede, meaning clarifies.

❧

The birth of meaning is an act of faith.

❧

Man was made for transcendence.

❧

Growth is the submission of man
into a purpose beyond his own.

❧

How can one teach a fish
the meaning of drowning?

❧

Our feet point in the same direction as our eyes.

❧

It takes but a candle to illumine the night.

❧

The flame points upward.

Beware of the panther who strides out of your dreams!

Ignorance and Vanity

The mask must fit the face,
not the face the mask.

※

It takes but a little silver
to turn glass into a mirror!

※

No face has the right to be upset with the mirror.

※

It is your own mask that creates the masks
around you.

※

Ignorance affirms the shadow while denying its cause.

We, who but traced the contours of the clouds,
imagined we possessed the sky!

Temptation and Desire

Beware of the panther who strides out
of your dreams!

❦

We are destroyed by the phantoms
we permit to be real.

❦

Temptation is a door whose handle
can only be turned by yourself.

❦

Has glitter made us forget the light by which we see?

❦

The skin of attachment must be shed
by the snake of desire.

❦

The target that seduces the archer's eye,
seduces the arrow also.

❦

The rose plucked the eyes
before the hand plucked the rose.

❦

To pluck a rose is to open a wound.

❦

Give us blood to mingle,
not scars to heal!

Struggle and Suffering

It is the crushed flower
who yields her fragrance.

※

Sometimes the sky in us must crack
before the healing rain can fall.

※

Suffering is the inability to sublimate pain.

※

Transcendence is the only home for suffering.

※

Some fish remember the ocean
only when they are gasping in the air.

It may take a storm to notice the sky.

Darkness struggles against light:
to open an eye requires great courage.

Who dares walk on water
must never fear to drown.

Who holds a candle to darkness
must not fear what the light reveals.

Armour gives no strength,
only protection.

Choices and Consequences

How far we fall when the heavens tumble
from our eyes!

❧

To destroy beauty is to destroy the soul.

❧

The pain we cause and the joy we give
find their final home within us.

❧

To turn a blind eye in the daylight
is to be tormented with open eyes at night.

❧

The hand of greed closes to itself.

Man pursues the pain from which he flees.

What is the fullness of the orchard
to one who cannot taste the sweetness of its fruit?

None is so lonely as the flower
in whom the garden does not live.

Virtue and Dignity

Man is the earth's
gateway to heaven.

❦

Virtue rests upon faith.

❦

The most precious pearl
cannot be possessed,
merely cast away.

❦

By curbing our wants,
we discover our needs.

❦

The purpose of abstention is not the elimination of want
but the deepening of desire.

❦

Love does not seek to pluck roses.

❦

The true extent of one's wealth
is measured by the act of giving.

❦

Even what we took was given,
but we lacked the humility to know.

❦

Humility cannot exist without wonder.

Patience opens beautiful flowers.

Rather compromise a rule
than sacrifice a principle.

The tongue bites harder than the teeth
that surround it.

It is the blunt nail that cracks the plaster.

So much in life matters,
if we only had the courage to let it!

Repentance and Forgiveness

Anyone can turn back,
but it takes humility to return.

❦

The ocean would wash one's sins
if only one would enter it.

❦

Repentance is mercy to oneself.

❦

To forgive is to cast out shadows from one's soul.

❦

Forgiveness is the only redemption.

It is the uncleansed passage that remains blocked.

Compassion and Mercy

Conscience is the eye of compassion.

❧

Some tears harden the heart,
others moisten the soul.

❧

Nothing is truly distant as long as one
can feel its pain.

❧

By discovering your eyes,
I learned the meaning of tears.

❧

The tears of a lover are sacred
because they flow from another's eyes.

The flame is the fire's way of weeping.

The candle weeps for the moth
who kisses her flame.

The pools of our tears
reflect the sky.

The compassion of the tree
allows her leaves to fall.

An eye that can contain the whole world
cannot hold a single tear that is real.

❦

The sky itself trembles
when a teardrop trembles in the eye.

❦

The fires that burn in hell
are tinged with the light of mercy.

How night vanishes when a lantern glows!

Exile and Longing

Though you blow out love's candle,
you can never quench her flame.

※

I have fallen in love with the distance between us
because it reminds me of you.

※

How long will the skies ignore
the flower that yearns to open?

※

Loneliness is not absence
but the presence of absence.

※

There is no distance nearer nor farther than longing.

❧

Closeness is distance made palpable.

❧

Pain is a mask of longing.

❧

Sometimes we plead with the silence
in order to hear its response.

❧

The tongue that burns in silence, screams.

❧

Emptiness is a weight I cannot bear.

❧

A need knows more than a want can tell.

❧

Need never questions itself.

❧

Thirst does not question the shape of the glass.

❧

What we cannot hold in our arms,
we hold even closer in our dreams.

❧

I who am shaped by the earth
am longing to be shaped by the sky.

❦

It is because the soil loves me
that I am reaching for the sky.

❦

Loneliness is a star
longing for the night to shine.

❦

It is the seed's desire
that makes the flower bloom.

❦

The desire to look over the edge is drawing me
closer to the precipice of my dreams.

❦

If you won't let me light your darkness,
at least let me share your night.

The ink of my veins has written you
upon the page of my dreams.

Freedom and Captivity

As great as the sky may be,
it cannot capture the wind.

❧

The wind cannot possess
a single grain of sand.

❧

Freedom consists not in being released
but in letting go.

❧

It is more accurate to say:
"When the heart is free there are no rules"
than it is to say:
"When there are no rules the heart is free."

❧

I was never so near as to hold you,
nor so far that you could set me free.

❧

In trying to capture you I have learned
how complete is my own captivity.

❧

Whoever holds you, is held by you;
who builds a wall, is its prisoner.

❧

The puppet only dances
when the fingers pull its strings.

❧

The shell that was once the pearl's innocence
is now the emblem of her vulnerability.

❦

Man destroys what is precious
by refusing to let it go.

❦

To accept one's limitations is to be free.

❦

To decenter is to violate freedom.

❦

Dignity is the only freedom.

Hope

Hope was born within a seed
long before her flower bloomed.

༒

It is out of mud and darkness
that the lotus flower blossoms.

༒

Hope may be abandoned,
but it was never born to die.

༒

The thread of hope can never be cut
merely by the hands of another.

Self and Other

I am learning to make friends
with the stranger I have become.

※

The door to oneself is through another.

※

We are merely translations of each other's lives.

※

We are like cloth
spun from a single thread.

※

Eyes were not meant to see themselves,
but lose themselves in another.

By looking through another's eyes,
the lover learns to see.

I who am surrounded by distances
sing only of bridges.

We are the soil in which only
the seed of another can grow.

What the soul seeks in herself,
she discovers in another.

The Beloved unveils herself only to the lover.

The lover knows the Beloved
the way the shadow knows the flame.

When the Centre discovers itself,
the Circle opens.

Independence and Interdependence

You may be the farthest bead in the rosary,
but it is the same thread that connects us all.

※

I held you the way the sky holds rain:
so heavy within me, I wept to let you go.

※

Shadows are evidence of light.

※

When the flame dances in the night,
night trembles in the dancing flame.

Trust and Dependence

The whole ocean lay before me,
but I needed your well to drink!

✧

No door is abandoned by its own opening.

✧

To love is to give oneself up
to open air, with wings.

Self-Surrender

To enter nothingness,
one must give everything.

❧

The drop that kisses the ocean, drowns.

❧

The footprint appears only when the foot departs.

❧

The river cannot flow
unless we become the riverbank to its flowing.

❧

The diver enters the ocean
only by shattering the pane which reflects him.

No lover learned to swim
before learning to drown.

If you wish to be a candle,
become first as wax in a flame.

When hearts yield to the night,
what need even for light?

The fires that burn in hell are tinged with the light of mercy.

Inwardness and Transcendence

The key and lamp are both within.

※

The ascent retraces the descent.

※

To ascend, one must journey deep.

※

The fire that consumes the universe
is lit by a spark from within.

※

A fish enters the ocean from within.

The horizon you cannot reach is within.

The lighted candle melts into itself.

The fire dies into the ashes of its flame.

Snowflakes fall to earth, and melt,
then rise to heaven, unseen.

Prayer and Silence

One must kiss the earth
to touch the sky.

※

No one can kiss the earth
who has not first learned to kneel.

※

Prayer is a gift we make
of ourselves to ourselves.

※

Forgive us that we still need
to pray so much with words!

First the word,
then the breath,
finally silence.

Silence is the cloak of mystery.

Meditation unveils silence.

I haven't found a silence yet
that didn't speak of something.

Silence incubates our deepest desires.

❦

Sometimes the silence between us is so vast,
I need an echo to hear your name.

❦

Some merely surrender speech,
others embrace silence.

❦

The silence that discovers itself is broken.

❦

If you let the silence within you sing to itself,
you will become its song.

Love

The ship of desire is wrecked
at the lighthouse of love.

❦

Speech celebrates silence.
Love is its echo.

❦

Love is the intimacy of mystery.

❦

Our hearts, like the candle's flame,
point us to heaven.

❦

Love that can ask how much, is not enough.

Love is the altar of sacrifice.
The mark of its axe is within you.

Man is the scar within which God hides:
love opens the wound.

Your eyes are scars through which love has bled.

If I must drown, then let it be
in the pools of your eyes!

Love is water, not glass:
Break a pane of water, it mends;
splinter glass, it remains broken.

❧

No mirror has yet learned
how to reflect love.

❧

Our heart is a vessel
only love can fill.

❧

There is a cure for my blindness
only your eyes can understand.

❧

The beauty of the Rose teaches the eyes to sigh.

❧

Perfect love embraces imperfection.

Wholeness and Harmony

The Whole cannot be without you!

∞

Man cannot discover order
without being at its centre.

∞

Harmony subsists in joy,
uniformity, in fear.

∞

No disequilibrium can change
the overall equilibrium.

Serenity

When the Rose blooms,
the Garden is everywhere.

※

Only you, in whose arms I dance,
know the stillness I feel.

※

The moonlit fish appears
when the ripples subside.

Transfiguration and Beauty

How night vanishes when a lantern glows!

✤

What is the night without a star to make it shine?

✤

What use are eyes that cannot illumine the night?

✤

Sometimes we must light a candle
to see the beauty of the night.

✤

Such darkness in the universe,
yet to a candle the whole world is light!

Union

First, I was a fish.
Then, its mouth.
Finally, water.

The ship of desire is wrecked at the lighthouse of love.

BIOGRAPHIES OF THE CONTRIBUTORS

M. Ali Lakhani is a scholar of traditional metaphysics, a barrister, jurist, writer and poet. His books include *The Sacred Foundations of Justice in Islam* (World Wisdom, Bloomington, 2006, an anthology of essays containing his prize-winning essay, 'The Metaphysics of Human Governance: Imam 'Ali, Truth and Justice', which was described by Seyyed Hossein Nasr as "among the best writings" on Imam 'Ali, and "obligatory reading"), *The Timeless Relevance of Traditional Wisdom* (World Wisdom, Bloomington, 2010, a selection of essays on metaphysics) and *Faith and Ethics: The Vision of the Ismaili Imamat* (I. B. Tauris in association with the Institute of Ismaili Studies, 2018, a survey of the ideas of the Aga Khan). In 1998, he founded *Sacred Web: A Journal of Tradition and Modernity* (www.sacredweb.com), a bi-annual journal addressing issues of the modern world from the perspective of traditional metaphysics. He lives in Vancouver, Canada, where he has practiced law for over four decades, and has the honour of being Queen's Counsel.

Nigel Jackson is an artist and illustrator with a long-standing interest in traditional symbolism, sacred aesthetics and the spiritual world-view of the High Middle Ages. He writes about aspects of symbolism, esoterism and Tradition. He is formally filiated within the orthodox religious life of Catholic Christianity. A frequent contributor to *Sacred Web*, his art, which draws from his study of traditional symbolism, is regularly featured on the covers of the journal. He lives in England.

BARRY MCDONALD (1951-2021), a contemplative and poet, is the author of *No Other Word* (London, 2020) and *The Eagle's Flight* (San Rafael, 2008). He is also the editor of *Every Branch in Me: Essays on the Meaning of Man* (Bloomington, 2002), *Seeing God Everywhere: Essays on Nature and the Sacred* (Bloomington, 2003) and is the co-editor with Patrick Laude of *Music of the Sky: An Anthology of Spiritual Poetry* (Bloomington, 2004). His poems have appeared in numerous journals in the US and abroad, including *Temenos Academy Review*, *Sophia*, *Sacred Web*, *Cross Currents*, and *Sufi Journal*.

First, I was a fish.
Then, its mouth.
Finally, water.

www.ingramcontent.com/pod-product-compliance
Lightning Source LLC
Chambersburg PA
CBHW042314150426
43201CB00001B/3